Lucas Dives Deep

Written by Jasmine Richards

Illustrated by Keenon Ferrell

Collins

Chapter 1

Lucas hated swimming. The waves made his ears feel like they were filled with glue.

His friends asked him to dive. Lucas said he could not do it.

When swimming was finished, Lucas's year group went to see a display for their school project.

"This display offers clues to life over 400 years ago!" Mrs Plume said.

Lucas spotted a statue of a king, a painting of fruit and a gold coin.

Alongside a chest, a painting of a child was displayed. He looked just like Lucas.

The tag said:

Expert diver from 1547.
No name on record.

The diver in the painting grinned.

Lucas gulped but grinned back.

"So, what are you waiting for then?" the diver said.
"You should come and join my crew!"

"How?" Lucas asked. "You are just a painting!"

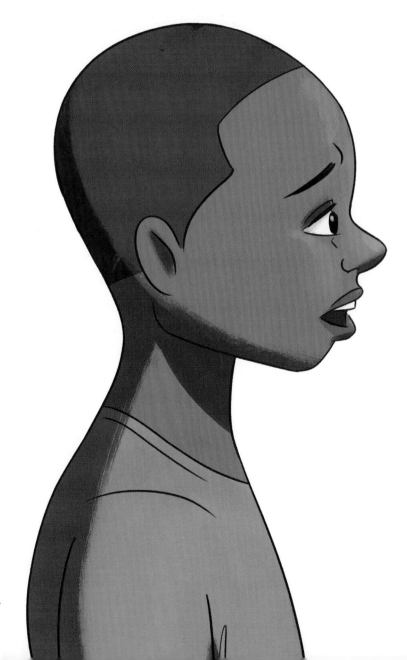

"That is true," the diver said, "but not for long.
Shall we go?"

Lucas nodded. The sea wind drew him off his feet and into the painting.

Then he was no longer in the room.

Chapter 3

Lucas was on a boat.

His legs felt odd, like they were made out of rubber.

"You will need to find your sea legs," said a person.

Lucas gazed at the diver from the painting. It was like looking at his twin.

"What is your name?" Lucas asked.

"I am from long ago," the diver said. "I need your help to find the king's coins. Let's dive."

Chapter 4

"To tell the truth, I'm not much of a swimmer," Lucas explained.

"Wow! Do you think I can be a fantastic diver as well?" Lucas asked.

The diver held out his hand. "Yes, I do. Come!"
They jumped into the blue sea.

Lucas swam with no fear. He glided over to a sparkling coin.

The coin flew Lucas back to the painting.
Now Lucas felt like a true expert diver, too!

People in the 1500s

Their stories are our stories.

trumpeter

farmer

diver

seamstress

⁂ After reading ⁂

Letters and Sounds: Phase 5

Word count: 364

Focus phonemes: /ai/ ay, a-e, ey /ee/ ie, ea /igh/ i-e, i /oa/ o /oo/ ue, ui, ew, ou, u, oul, u-e

Common exception words: of, to, the, into, are, my, he, we, be, said, do, were, when, what, school, our, their, people, Mrs, friends, your, out, was, come, asked

Curriculum links: PSHE; History

National Curriculum learning objectives: Reading/word reading: apply phonic knowledge and skills as the route to decode words; read accurately by blending sounds in unfamiliar words containing GPCs that have been taught; read common exception words, noting unusual correspondences between spelling and sound and where these occur in words; Reading/comprehension (KS2): understand what they read, in books they can read independently, by checking that the text makes sense to them, discussing their understanding and explaining the meaning of words in context; by drawing inferences such as inferring characters' feelings, thoughts and motives for their actions, and justifying inferences with evidence

Developing fluency

- Take turns to read a page. Check that your child uses a variety of tones, and different voices for the characters.

Phonic practice

- Ask your child to reread page 29 and find four words with different spellings of the /oo/ sound (*flew*, *Lucas*, *true*, *too*).
- Challenge your child to read these words and identify the spellings of the /oo/ sounds.

  clues (*ue*)   blew (*ew*)   fruit (*ui*)   you (*ou*)   should (*oul*)

Extending vocabulary

- Discuss the meaning of each of the words below in the context of each page. Challenge your child to think of a word with a similar meaning (synonym) for each.

  page 19: odd (e.g. *strange*)   page 26: fantastic (e.g. *amazing*)
  page 28: sparkling (e.g. *glinting*)